# ADVENT and CHRISTMAS
## ——— with ———
# THE SAINTS

*Anthony F. Chiffolo*

Liguori

LIGUORI, MISSOURI

*To Rusty and Lisa*

*Imprimi Potest:* Richard Thibodeau, C.Ss.R., Provincial, Denver Province, The Redemptorists

Published by Liguori Publications, Liguori, Missouri
www.liguori.org
www.catholicbooksonline.com

**Library of Congress Cataloging-in-Publication Data**

Chiffolo, Anthony F., 1959–
    Advent and Christmas with the Saints / Anthony F. Chiffolo.
        p. cm.
    ISBN 0-7648-0993-8
    1. Advent—Prayer-books and devotions—English. 2. Christmas—Prayer-books and devotions—English. 3. Devotional calendars—Catholic Church. 4. Catholic Church—Prayer-books and devotions—English. I. Title.

BX2170.A4C48 2003
242'.33—dc21                                                                              2003047411

The editor and publisher gratefully acknowledge permission to reprint/reproduce copyrighted works granted by the publishers/sources listed on pages 99–102.

Printed in the United States of America
07 06 05 04 03   5 4 3 2 1
First edition

# Advent and Christmas
## with
### THE SAINTS

# $\mathcal{C}$ontents

# *Epigraph*

MY SOUL, have you found what you are looking for? You were looking for God, and you have discovered that he is the supreme being, and that you could not possibly imagine anything more perfect. You have discovered that this supreme being is life itself, light, wisdom, goodness, eternal blessedness and blessed eternity.

*SAINT ANSELM OF CANTERBURY (1033–1109)*

# Introduction

IT'S A TRUISM that almost all of us are too busy to pay proper attention to our spiritual lives. I am no exception. So I welcomed the opportunity to write this book, as the assignment came to me in the fall and I anticipated being able to spend my own Advent and Christmas seasons in working on it. Alas, my own busyness overwhelmed my good intentions. It was not shopping or decorating that got in the way, but bible classes and "lessons and carols" and seasonal family activities, which just seemed to pile one upon another until Advent and Christmas were filled to overflowing with good news that left no time for writing.

So I present this book with a certain amount of trepidation. Who am I to dare advise anyone about how to approach this time of year? Let me, rather, follow the Baptist's example, stepping aside to allow the saints themselves to speak, to guide our thoughts toward the birth of the promised One and what that coming means to us today.

We can begin our time of preparation with the words of the Baptist himself: "Change your hearts and minds, for the reign of heaven is about to break in upon you!" (Matthew 3:2). Will it happen this Christmas, that God will crash in upon us, like a tidal wave, tearing us from our moorings and drawing us into the deep? And if so, how can the four short weeks of Advent possibly prepare our souls for such a cataclysm?

Will it be so dramatic? Frances Xavier Cabrini wrote, "The Holy Spirit descends upon us with great gentleness, never with a racket." Perhaps God's coming will be a quiet event, barely noticed, because God is already with us. Katharine Drexel taught her sisters, "We bear God within our souls…," and Teresa of Ávila, repeating what the Spirit had revealed to her, advised, "In yourself seek Me." But we do seek God, ardently. As Henry Suso exclaimed, "My soul has longed for you all night…!"

If we ever do find God, what then? Our inclination is to mumble a quick song of praise, drop our gifts before the manger, and rush back to our own busy lives, carrying with us only a vague recollection of that glorious night when the heavens rang and we finally perceived the Divine. Might we dare to remain with Immanuel, as the saints did? "One thing is necessary: to be near Jesus," Padre Pio believed, because with God nearby, anything is possible.

The saints had many astounding things to say about the Incarnation. In this book, we'll walk day by day through Advent and the Christmas season with some of the greatest spiritual sages of Christianity: prophets like Mary, the Mother of Jesus, apostles like Paul, mystics like Gertrude, stigmatists like Francis, bishops like Ambrose, anchorites like Julian, popes like John, scholars like Thomas, and activists like Teresa. Considering their thoughts anew might challenge our preconceived ideas about the meaning of the season, leading us out of our comfortableness and into the transforming presence of the Spirit, where we repeat along with Catherine of Siena, "You, O eternal Trinity, are a deep sea, into which the more I enter the more I find, and the more I find the more I seek." From the forty saints who speak in this book, we can learn about the deepest desires of our hearts, about believing in something beyond ourselves, and about what we can and must do to convert our hearts and minds and establish the kindom of God now, in our families and in our communities.

Perhaps it is enough to pray along with Alphonsus, "Let us ask light of Jesus Christ and of his most holy mother, and so let us begin."

Although I personally believe that God is neither male nor female and have, thus, used inclusive, gender-neutral language to refer to God, many of the saints adhered to a different view. I have retained their usage when quoting them. Likewise, I have retained the saints' patriarchal language, though I have avoided it in my own writing.

Similarly, I have used the word *kindom* instead of the more traditional *kingdom*, as the former avoids the sexist and elitist connotations of the latter. Also, the sense of God's family represented by *kindom* reflects the centrality of the Christian message of hospitality that *kingdom* may not.

# How to Use This Book

ADVENT—that period of great anticipatory joy—is a time of preparation for the celebration of Christ's arrival in Bethlehem as a helpless infant. In the Western liturgy, Advent begins four Sundays prior to December 25—the Sunday closest to November 30 which is the feast of Saint Andrew, one of Jesus' first disciples. The annual commemoration of Christ's birth begins the Christmas cycle of the liturgical year—a cycle which runs from Christmas Eve to the Sunday after the feast of the Epiphany. In keeping with the unfolding of the message of the liturgical year, this book is designed to be used during the entire period from the first Sunday of Advent to the end of the Christmas cycle. The four weeks of Advent are often thought of as symbolizing the four different ways that Christ comes into the world: (1) at his birth as a helpless infant at Bethlehem; (2) at his arrival in the hearts of believers; (3) at his death; and (4) at his arrival on Judgment Day.

Because Christmas falls on a different day of the week each year, the fourth week of Advent is never really finished; it is abruptly, joyously, and solemnly abrogated by the annual coming again of Christ at Christmas. Christ's Second Coming will also one day abruptly interrupt our sojourn here on earth.

Since the calendar dictates the number of days in Advent, this book includes Scripture and meditation readings for a full twenty-eight days. These twenty-eight daily readings make up Part I of this book. It is suggested that the reader begin at the beginning and, on Christmas, switch to Part II, which contains materials for the twelve days of Christmas. If there are any "extra" entries from Part I, these may be read by doubling up days, if so desired, or by reading two entries on weekends. Alternately, one may just skip these entries that do not fit within the Advent time frame for that particular year.

Part III of this book proposes two optional formats for using each daily entry as part of a longer liturgical observance similar to Night Prayer combined with a version of the Office of Readings. These options are for those who may wish to use this book as part of a more-developed individual or group observance. The purpose of these readings is to enrich the Advent/Christmas/Epiphany season of the liturgical year and set up a means by which individuals, families, or groups may observe the true meaning of the season.

# PART I

~~~~~~

# READINGS *for* ADVENT

# DAY 1

The time is surely coming, says the LORD,
when the one who plows shall overtake the one who reaps,
and the treader of grapes the one who sows the seed;
the mountains shall drip sweet wine,
and all the hills shall flow with it.
I will restore the fortunes of my people Israel,
and they shall rebuild the ruined cities and inhabit them;
they shall plant vineyards and drink their wine,
and they shall make gardens and eat their fruit.
I will plant them upon their land,
and they shall never again be plucked up
out of the land that I have given them,
says the LORD your God.

AMOS 9:13–15

# O God of Promise!

*Thus was I taught by the grace of God that I should stead-fastly hold myself in the faith as I had before understood it, and that I should seriously believe that all manner of things would be well, as our Lord at that same time had showed me. For by the great deed that our Lord shall do He shall save His word in all things and He shall make well all that is not well—though how it shall be done no creature below Christ knows or shall know until it is done. This is what I understood from what our Lord communicated to me at this time.*

SAINT JULIAN OF NORWICH (1342–141?)

❖ ❖ ❖

This is the day that you have made, O God of Promise, and your psalmist has instructed me to be glad in it. For like all days, today is a day of possibilities, and if I allow it, your loving Spirit will reveal the day's magnificence. Yet today is also a day of special promise, for it is the beginning of my Advent pilgrimage, my preparation for the Incarnation of your loving Spirit in the Messiah. As I proceed on this pilgrimage, help me perceive where I need to rebuild, revise, replant, and restore. Help me remove what is blocking my vision of you, reaffirm my commitment to love, and rejoice in the goodness of creation. And help me remember that your loving care will make well all that is not well in my life, transforming my Advent efforts into a journey of glory. Amen.

# DAY 2

*See, I am sending my messenger to prepare the way before me, and the Lord whom you seek will suddenly come to his temple. The messenger of the covenant in whom you delight—indeed, he is coming, says the LORD of hosts. But who can endure the day of his coming, and who can stand when he appears?*

*For he is like a refiner's fire and like fullers' soap; he will sit as a refiner and purifier of silver, and he will purify the descendants of Levi and refine them like gold and silver, until they present offerings to the LORD in righteousness. Then the offering of Judah and Jerusalem will be pleasing to the LORD as in the days of old and as in former years.*

MALACHI 3:1–4

# O God of Purification!

*T*he Jews solemnized a day called by them *dies ignis,* the day of fire with which Nehemias consumed the sacrifice, upon his return with his countrymen from the captivity of Babylon. Even so, and indeed with more reason, should Christmas day be called the day of fire, on which a God came as a little child to cast the fire of love into the hearts of men. "I came to cast fire on the earth." So spoke Jesus Christ, and truly so it was….

It is a custom with many Christians to anticipate the arrival of Christmas…by fitting up in their homes a crib to represent the birth of Jesus Christ; but there are few who think of preparing their hearts, so that the infant Jesus may be born in them…. Among these few, however, we would be reckoned, in order that we too may be made worthy to burn with that happy flame which gives contentment to souls on this earth, and bliss in heaven. Let us consider…how the eternal Word had no other end in becoming man than to inflame us with his divine love. Let us ask light of Jesus Christ and of his most holy mother, and so let us begin.

*SAINT ALPHONSUS LIGUORI (1696–1787)*

❖ ❖ ❖

O God of Purification, here I am at the beginning of my Advent journey, yet already I feel overwhelmed with holiday anxieties. O Living Flame, refine my to-do list, that I might put first what I must do to welcome you into my life once again. Clarify my desires, that I might undertake only what you call me to in this season. And purify my intentions, that I might begin right now to put myself under your loving guidance. Amen.

## ░ DAY 3 ░

*Six months later, the angel Gabriel was sent from God to a town in Galilee called Nazareth, to a young woman named Mary.... Upon arriving, the angel said to Mary, "Rejoice, highly favored one! God is with you! Blessed are you among women!"*

*Mary was deeply troubled by these words and wondered what the angel's greeting meant. The angel went on to say to her, "Don't be afraid, Mary. You have found favor with God. You'll conceive and bear a son, and give him the name Jesus— 'Deliverance.' His dignity will be great, and he will be called the Only Begotten of God. God will give Jesus the judgment seat of David, his ancestor, to rule over the house of Jacob forever, and his reign will never end."*

*Mary said to the angel, "How can this be, since I have never been with a man?"*

*The angel answered her, "The Holy Spirit will come upon you, and the power of the Most High will overshadow you—*

*hence the offspring to be born will be called the Holy One of God. Know too that Elizabeth, your kinswoman, has conceived a child in her old age; she who was thought to be infertile is now in her sixth month. Nothing is impossible with God."*

*Mary said, "I am the servant of God. Let it be done to me as you say."*

LUKE 1:26–38

## *O God of Possibilities!*

*I* will abandon myself fully to the Holy Spirit, allowing myself to be led wherever and whenever the Spirit wants, accompanying the Spirit, for my part, with effective and strong resolutions and serious discernment....The Holy Spirit descends upon us with great gentleness, never with a racket.

*SAINT FRANCES XAVIER CABRINI (1850–1917)*

✣ ✣ ✣

Dear God, why do I await a telephone call, a letter, an e-mail, or even an angel to announce your intentions? I am so afraid of responsibility, for my decisions, my actions, my very words and thoughts might lead me to catastrophe. O God of Possibilities, teach me to recognize that your Spirit is already quietly at work in my life. Help me trust that your Spirit is already informing my decisions, guiding my actions, and forming my words and thoughts. I pray that, with your grace, I might bravely cooperate with you in bringing your infinite possibilities into reality. Amen.

# DAY 4

*Within a few days Mary set out and hurried to the hill country
to a town of Judah, where she entered Zechariah's house and
greeted Elizabeth.*

*As soon as Elizabeth heard Mary's greeting, the child leaped
in her womb and Elizabeth was filled with the Holy Spirit. In
a loud voice she exclaimed, "Blessed are you among women,
and blessed is the fruit of your womb! But why am I so favored, that the mother of the Messiah should come to me? The
moment your greeting reached my ears, the child in my womb
leaped for joy. Blessed is she who believed that what Our God
said to her would be accomplished!"*

*Mary said: "My soul proclaims your greatness, O God,
and my spirit rejoices in you, my Savior...."*

LUKE 1:39–47

# O God of Rejoicing!

When John leaps for joy Elizabeth is filled with the Holy Spirit, but we know that though Mary's spirit rejoices she does not need to be filled with the Holy Spirit. Her son, who is beyond our understanding, is active in his mother in a way beyond our understanding. Elizabeth is filled with the Holy Spirit after conceiving John, while Mary is filled with the Holy Spirit before conceiving the Lord. Elizabeth says: *Blessed are you because you have believed.*

You also are blessed because you have heard and believed. A soul that believes both conceives and brings forth the Word of God and acknowledges his works.

Let Mary's soul be in each of you to proclaim the greatness of the Lord. Let her spirit be in each to rejoice in the Lord. Christ has only one mother in the flesh, but we all bring forth Christ in faith.

SAINT AMBROSE OF MILAN (C. 340–397)

✤ ✤ ✤

Just as Mary desired a sign to verify the presence of the Divine within herself, so I too sometimes need outward signs to remind me that God is present within. O God of Rejoicing, open my heart, that I might recognize the fortuitous signs you have placed before me. Touch my soul, that I might respond with rejoicing to the wonders of your abiding love. Most of all, infuse me with your Spirit, that I too might bring forth the Word of God into the world. Amen.

# DAY 5

The LORD created me at the beginning of his work,
   the first of his acts of long ago.
      Ages ago I was set up,
   at the first, before the beginning of the earth.
When there were no depths I was brought forth,
when there were no springs abounding with water....
   When he established the heavens, I was there,
      when he drew a circle on the face of the deep,
         when he made firm the skies above,
      when he established the fountains of the deep,
         when he assigned to the sea its limit,
   so that the waters might not transgress his command,
when he marked out the foundations of the earth,
      then I was beside him, like a master worker;
         and I was daily his delight,
            rejoicing before him always,

*rejoicing in his inhabited world*
*and delighting in the human race.*

PROVERBS 8:22–31

# O Sophia!

*Y*ou, O eternal Trinity, are a deep sea, into which the more I enter the more I find, and the more I find the more I seek. The soul cannot be satiated in your abyss, for she continually hungers after you, the eternal Trinity, desiring to see you with the light of your light. As the hart desires the springs of living water, so my soul desires to leave the prison of this dark body and see you in truth.

O abyss, O eternal Godhead, O sea profound, what more could you give me than yourself! You are the fire that ever burns without being consumed; you consume in your heat all the soul's self-love; you are the fire which takes away cold; with your light you illuminate me so that I may know all your truth. Clothe me, clothe me with yourself, Eternal Truth, so that I may run this mortal life with true obedience, and with the light of your most holy faith.

SAINT CATHERINE OF SIENA (1347–1380)

✢ ✢ ✢

O Sophia, I long to drink from your eternal well. My soul is an arid place, in need of God's life-giving Spirit: quench my thirst, so that my desert might bloom. My soul is a frozen place, in need of God's blazing love: warm my heart, so that my winter might thaw. My soul is a dark place, in need of God's shining wisdom: open my eyes, so that my sight might be restored. Give me a clear vision of my way back to God, along with the courage and strength to continue the journey. Amen.

## DAY 6

*"I've come to light a fire on the earth.
How I wish the blaze were ignited already!"*

LUKE 12:49

*You made the night your cloak;
you covered yourself in a canopy of storm clouds.*

PSALM 18:11

# O God of Darkness!

Come, my Light, and illumine my darkness.

Come, my Life, and revive me from death.

Come, my Physician, and heal my wounds.

Come, Flame of divine love, and burn up the thorns of my sins, kindling my heart with the flame of thy love.

Come, my King, sit upon the throne of my heart and reign there. For thou alone art my King and my Lord.

*SAINT DIMITRII OF ROSTOV (1641–1709)*

✦ ✦ ✦

I often forget that because you are God of All Things you are certainly God of Darkness as well. So why do I plead to be led out of my darkness? You are with me always, even in my deepest pit, calling me, loving me, just as you have promised. O God of Darkness, I pray that I might find you in the darknesses of my life, in those moments when I am blind to the beauty of creation, when I am frozen to the love of community, when I am lost to your abiding presence. Amen.

## DAY 7

*He said, "Go out and stand on the mountain before the LORD, for the LORD is about to pass by." Now there was a great wind, so strong that it was splitting mountains and breaking rocks in pieces before the LORD, but the LORD was not in the wind; and after the wind an earthquake, but the LORD was not in the earthquake; and after the earthquake a fire, but the LORD was not in the fire; and after the fire a sound of sheer silence. When Elijah heard it, he wrapped his face in his mantle and went out and stood at the entrance of the cave. Then there came a voice to him....*

1 KINGS 19:11–13

# O God of Silence!

Fire of the Spirit, life of the lives of creatures,
   spiral of sanctity, bond of all natures,
      glow of charity, lights of clarity,
      taste of sweetness to sinners—
      be with us and hear us.
Composer of all things, light of all the risen,
      key of salvation, release from the dark prison,
      hope of all unions, scope of chastities,
      joy in the glory, strong honor—
      be with us and hear us.

*SAINT HILDEGARD OF BINGEN (1098–1179)*

✢ ✢ ✢

This Advent journey is already a week gone, and I've seen a whirlwind of new commitments, an earthquake of altered plans, a fire of "emergency" visits and shopping and decorating—but very little silence. Dear God, if you were with me in any infinitesimal moments of sheer silence, then I'm sorry I missed you, because I was not "silent" myself. O God of Silence, quiet my busy, noisy soul, that I might finally recognize, accept, and enjoy your constant, sometimes silent presence by my side. Amen.

# DAY 8

*My people, hear my teaching;*
*listen to the words of my mouth!*
*I will open my mouth in parables,*
*I will utter things hidden from of old—*
*the things we have heard and known,*
*things our ancestors have told us.*
*We won't hide them from our children,*
*we will tell the next generation.*

*We'll tell them of your praiseworthy deeds, Adonai,*
*your power, and the wonders you have performed....*

*Then they would put their trust in you*
*and not forget your deeds, but keep your commandments....*

PSALM 78:1–7

# O God of Wonders!

One of his [Nicholas's] neighbors, a nobleman, was so poor that he planned to deliver his three daughters to prostitution in order to make a living from the profits of their shame.

When Nicholas heard of this, he was horrified at the thought of such a sin. Wrapping a lump of gold in a cloth, during the night he threw it through a window in his neighbor's house. Then he fled without being seen. The next morning the man found the bundle of gold. Thanking God, he immediately arranged for his eldest daughter's marriage....

A few days later a bundle of gold twice as large was thrown into his house. He heard the noise it made falling and set out in pursuit of Nicholas. He begged him to stop so he could see his face. He ran so fast that he caught up with the young man and recognized him. Throwing himself before him, he tried to kiss his feet. But Nicholas declined his thanks. He exacted a promise that the man would keep the secret of his deed until after his death.

*SAINT NICHOLAS OF MYRA (D. 342) AS TOLD BY JACOB OF VORAGINE*

✛ ✛ ✛

O God of Wonders, I praise your name for the gifts you have bestowed upon me, especially those secret and unexpected presents that have raised my spirits and gladdened my heart in difficult times. I promise to take time this day to tell my family and friends about the wonderful things I've experienced—during either this or previous Advent and Christmas seasons. I thank you and praise you for these many blessings—and for those yet to come. Amen.

# DAY 9

*"You are the light of the world. You don't build a city on a hill, then try to hide it, do you? You don't light a lamp, then put it under a bushel basket, do you? No, you set it on a stand where it gives light to all in the house. In the same way, your light must shine before others so that they may see your good acts and give praise to your Abba God in heaven."*

MATTHEW 5:14–16

# O God of Light!

Lead, kindly Light, amid the encircling gloom,
    Lead thou me on!
    The night is dark, and I am far from home,
        Lead thou me on!
    Keep thou my feet! I do not ask to see
    The distant scene; one step enough for me.

*VENERABLE JOHN HENRY NEWMAN (1801–1890)*

❖ ❖ ❖

O God of Light, why do I seek outside sources of spiritual illumination? Remind me that, made in your image, I have your very light within me, from the moment of my creation, and that this divine inner light, the light of my own soul, has power to shine to the ends of the earth, to illuminate my path to you, and to guide others along their way to you too. Keep this light burning brightly within me, I pray, that I might never lose my way, and so that everyone I encounter today might recognize your Spirit in my soul. Amen.

# DAY 10

*God is our refuge and our strength,*
*who from of old has helped us in our distress.*
*Therefore we fear nothing—*
*even if the earth should open up in front of us*
*and mountains plunge into the depths of the sea,*
*even if the earth's waters rage and foam*
*and the mountains tumble with its heaving....*

Adonai Sabaoth is with us—
our stronghold is the God of Israel!

PSALM 46:1–3, 7

# O God of Fullness!

*D*uring painful times, when you feel a terrible void, think how God is enlarging the capacity of your soul so that it can receive him—making it, as it were, infinite as he is infinite. Look upon each pain as a love token coming to you directly from God in order to unite you to him.

*BLESSED ELIZABETH OF THE TRINITY (1880–1906)*

❖ ❖ ❖

O God of Fullness, Advent and Christmas events sometimes conjure painful memories of times past when these holidays were not so pleasant, and the dread of revisiting them paralyzes me. Heal my old hurts, I pray, easing my pain with your balm, replacing my hatreds with your love, and filling my emptiness with your infinite fullness, that I might move forward in joy to greet your coming. Amen.

# DAY 11

*"Don't store up earthly treasures for yourselves, which moths and rust destroy and thieves can break in and steal. But store up treasures for yourselves in heaven, where neither moth nor rust can destroy them and thieves cannot break in and steal them. For where your treasure is, there will your heart be as well."*

MATTHEW 6:19–21

# O God of Heavenly Treasure!

*G*rant to us, O Lord, not to mind earthly things, but rather to love heavenly things, that while all things around us pass away, we even now may hold fast those things that abide forever.

*SAINT LEO THE GREAT (D. 461)*

✦ ✦ ✦

My holidays are filled with rituals that have become comfortable, enjoyable traditions: baking cookies, choosing the tree, decorating the house, wrapping gifts, sending cards. But sometimes I wonder if these rituals have taken over, if they have become the very purpose of my life during the Advent and Christmas seasons. O God of Heavenly Treasure, help me put my holiday customs in proper perspective, that I might focus not on these rituals that pass away but, rather, on the Love-coming-into-the-world that abides forever. Amen.

## DAY 12

*There is in her a spirit that is intelligent, holy,*
*unique, manifold, subtle,*
*mobile, clear, unpolluted,*
*distinct, invulnerable, loving the good, keen,*
*irresistible, beneficent, humane,*
*steadfast, sure, free from anxiety,*
*all-powerful, overseeing all,*
*and penetrating through all spirits*
*that are intelligent, pure, and altogether subtle.*
*For wisdom is more mobile than any motion;*
*because of her pureness she pervades and*
*penetrates all things.*
*For she is a breath of the power of God,*
*and a pure emanation of the glory of the Almighty;*
*therefore nothing defiled gains entrance into her.*

*For she is a reflection of eternal light,*
*a spotless mirror of the working of God,*
*and an image of his goodness.*

WISDOM OF SOLOMON 7:22–26

## O Immaculate Conception!

*A* golden hour was my conception, for then began the principle of the salvation of all, and darkness hastened to light. God wished to do in His work something singular and hidden from the world, as He did in the dry rod blooming. But know that my conception was not known to all, because God wished that as the natural law and the voluntary election of good and bad preceded the written law, and the written law followed, restraining all inordinate notions, so it pleased God, that His friends should piously doubt of my conception, and that each should show his zeal till the truth became clear in its preordained time.

THE IMMACULATE CONCEPTION,
AS REVEALED TO SAINT BIRGITTA OF SWEDEN (1303–1373)

✤ ✤ ✤

O Immaculate Conception, the mysteries of the Christmas story are revealed through your experience, yet they are completely incomprehensible to my mortal understanding. Most Blessed of Women, infuse my soul with your grace, I pray, that I might put aside my natural skepticism and begin to apprehend the miraculous beauty of your life and your marvelous role in God's eternal plan. Amen.

# DAY 13

*Sing for joy, O heavens, and exult, O earth;*
*break forth, O mountains, into singing!*
*For the LORD has comforted his people,*
*and will have compassion on his suffering ones.*

ISAIAH 49:13

## O God of Exultation!

My soul proclaims your greatness, O God,
    and my spirit rejoices in you, my Savior.
For you have looked with favor
        upon your lowly servant,
and from this day forward
        all generations will call me blessed.

For you, the Almighty, have done great things for me,
    and holy is your Name.
Your mercy reaches from age to age
    for those who fear you.
You have shown strength with your arm,
    you have scattered the proud in their conceit,
you have deposed the mighty from their thrones
    and raised the lowly to high places.
You have filled the hungry with good things,
    while you have sent the rich away empty.
You have come to the aid of Israel your servant,
    mindful of your mercy—
the promise you made to our ancestors—
    to Sarah and Abraham
    and their descendants forever.

*SAINT MARY, THE MOTHER OF JESUS (FIRST CENTURY)*

✤ ✤ ✤

Do I exult in you as I want you to exult in me?
Forgive me, O God of Exultation, for in my rising moments I have neglected to praise you for the glorious promises of the dawning day. Forgive me, O God of Exultation, for in my daily moments I have neglected to love you for your presence in the abiding day. Forgive me, O God of Exultation, for in my resting moments I have neglected to thank you for the blessings of the setting day. Pardon my selfish shortsightedness, and bless me anew, I pray, that I might learn from Mary, the Mother of your Son, to praise you for the great things you have done for me. Amen.

# DAY 14

*Our knowledge is imperfect and our prophesying is imperfect. When the perfect comes, the imperfect will pass away....Now we see indistinctly, as in a mirror; then we will see face to face. My knowledge is imperfect now; then I will know even as I am known.*

1 CORINTHIANS 13:9–12

## O God of Mystery!

Our Lady, while she awaits the birth of her Child, appears to us as a perfect mystery of recollection and absorption in God. She bears the wonder of God below her heart; she is conscious He dwells within her and she is full of tranquil faith in the angel's message, in the signs of the nearness of the approaching Savior whom even she does not behold yet.

In the same way our own inner world conceals a wealth of sacred mysteries. We bear God within our souls by grace and with Him the kingdom of heaven and eternal life. All this dwells within us, although to us it is invisible. Yet we must not yield to doubt and wavering because we cannot see God. His traces are there for us to see in the whole creation, giving fresh life and growth everywhere. *We live in the midst of innumerable mysteries, which are to be solved by faith alone.* These reflections should constantly spur us to fresh activity and increase our joy in God, while banishing all melancholy and dejection.

*SAINT KATHARINE DREXEL (1858–1955)*

✦ ✦ ✦

O God of Mystery, where is the One who has been promised, the One who will solve all mysteries and answer all questions? The lengthening nights of Advent darken any glimmer of hope. Despair lurks around each corner; fear and doubt overwhelm me; and my faith flees. Only a faint remnant of trust sustains me—a childlike belief in the beauty of a mystery that I cannot understand, the mystery of how your unconditional love for me will bring my joy to fruition. Though I may never fully understand your ways, may I now find my peace in abandoning myself to your care. Amen.

# DAY 15

*I'm always aware of your presence;*
*you are right by my side, and nothing can shake me.*
*My heart is happy and my tongue sings for joy;*
*I feel completely safe with you,*
*because you won't abandon me to the Grave;*
*you won't let your loved one see decay.*
*You show me the path to Life;*
*your presence fills me with joy,*
*and by your side I find enduring pleasure.*

PSALM 16:8–11

# O Eternal Life!

*I* pray you, noble Jesus, that as you have graciously granted me joyfully to imbibe the words of your knowledge, so you will also of your bounty grant me to come at length to yourself, the fount of all wisdom, and to dwell in your presence forever.

*SAINT BEDE (673–735)*

✦ ✦ ✦

O Eternal Life, the source of my being and the goal of my existence, to you I need to return, with you I long to be, in you I desire to rest. Just as the prodigal feels upended when away from home, so I am rootless when I am not in your presence. Lead me back, I pray, to the bedrock of your love, that I might once again find my true dwelling place in joyful reunion with you. Amen.

# DAY 16

*"Therefore the Lord himself will give you a sign. Look, the young woman is with child and shall bear a son, and shall name him Immanuel. He shall eat curds and honey by the time he knows how to refuse the evil and choose the good."*

ISAIAH 7:14–15

# O Mother of the Incarnation!

*M*y dear little son, I love you. I desire you to know who I am. I am the ever-virgin Mary, Mother of the true God who gives life and maintains its existence. He created all things. He is in all places. He is Lord of Heaven and Earth....I am your merciful Mother, the Mother of all who live united in this land, and of all mankind, and of all those who love me, of those who cry to me, of those who have confidence in me. Here I will see their tears; I will console them and they will be at peace....Do not be distressed, my littlest son. Am I not here with you who am your Mother? Are you not under my shadow and protection? Am I not of your kind?

*OUR LADY OF GUADALUPE, AS TOLD TO BLESSED JUAN DIEGO*
*(SIXTEENTH CENTURY)*

✢ ✢ ✢

O Mother of the Incarnation, were you ever as divinely confused as I am about what it means to incarnate God? Lead me, dear Mother, closer to your divine Son, teaching me the true meaning of Incarnation. Please guide me, I pray, with the same wisdom with which you guided Immanuel, that I might choose your Son's way and bring God's love into the world anew. Amen.

# DAY 17

*Put on the full armor of God so that you can stand firm against the tactics of the Devil. Our battle ultimately is not against human forces, but against the sovereignties and powers, the rulers of the world of darkness, and the evil spirits of the heavenly realms. You must put on the armor of God if you are to resist on the evil day and, having done everything you can, to hold your ground. Stand fast then, with truth as the belt around your waist, justice as your breastplate, and zeal to spread the Good News of peace as your footgear. In all circumstances, hold faith up before you as your shield; it will help you extinguish the fiery darts of the Evil One. Put on the helmet of salvation, and carry the sword of the Spirit, which is the word of God.*

EPHESIANS 6:11–17

# O God of Hosts!

I arise today
   with God's strength to pilot me:
      God's might to uphold me
      God's wisdom to guide me
      God's eye to look ahead for me
      God's ear to hear me
      God's word to speak for me
      God's hand to defend me
      God's way to lie before me
      God's shield to protect me
      God's host to safeguard me....

*SAINT PATRICK (ATTRIBUTED)*

❖ ❖ ❖

O God of Hosts, this season of preparation has drained my spirits, and your coming seems still a distant promise. As I weary of the rush and anticipation of Advent, I already long for the serene quiet of Epiphany. Please, God, send your angels to uphold my soul and reinforce my resolve to persevere on this journey, that I might, like the Magi, come into your presence at last. Amen.

# DAY 18

*A voice cries out:*
*"In the wilderness prepare the way of the Lord,*
*make straight in the desert a highway for our God.*
*Every valley shall be lifted up,*
*and every mountain and hill be made low;*
*the uneven ground shall become level,*
*and the rough places a plain.*
*Then the glory of the Lord shall be revealed,*
*and all people shall see it together,*
*for the mouth of the Lord has spoken."*

Isaiah 40:3–5

# O Rising Sun!

Blessed are you, the Most High God of Israel—
    for you have visited and redeemed your people.
    You have raised up a mighty savior for us
        of the house of David,
    as you promised through the mouths of your holy ones,
        the prophets from ancient times....
And you, my child, will be called
    the prophet of the Most High,
for you'll go before Our God
    to prepare the way for the Promised One,
giving the people the knowledge of salvation
    through forgiveness of their sins.
Such is the tender mercy of our God,
    who from on high
    will bring the Rising Sun to visit us,
to give light to those who live
    in darkness and the shadow of death
and to guide our feet
    into the way of peace.

SAINT ZECHARIAH (FIRST CENTURY)

✤ ✤ ✤

When comes the dawn, O Rising Sun? My night is deep, and I am afraid of its enduring. Please send me a morning star, some herald of your coming, that I might persist in hope and continue to believe in the nearness of your living presence. Amen.

# ※※※ DAY 19 ※※※

*Yet even now, says the LORD,*
*return to me with all your heart,*
*with fasting, with weeping, and with mourning;*
*rend your hearts and not your clothing.*
*Return to the LORD, your God,*
*for he is gracious and merciful,*
*slow to anger, and abounding in steadfast love,*
*and relents from punishing.*

JOEL 2:12–13

## O Good News!

ohn said to the crowds who came out to be baptized by him, "You pack of snakes! Who warned you to escape the wrath to come? Produce good fruit as a sign of your repentance. And don't presume to say to yourselves, 'We have Sarah and Abraham as our mother and father,' for I tell you that God can raise children for Sarah and Abraham from these very stones. The ax is already laid at the root of the tree; every tree that doesn't produce good fruit will be cut down and tossed into the fire."

When the people asked him, "What should we do?" John replied, "Let the one with two coats share with the one who has none. Let those who have food do the same."...

The people were full of anticipation, wondering in their hearts whether John might be the Messiah. John answered them all by saying, "I am baptizing you in water, but someone is coming who is mightier than I, whose sandals I am not fit to untie! This One will baptize you in the Holy Spirit and in fire. A winnowing-fan is in his hand to clear the threshing floor and gather the wheat into the granary, but the chaff will be burnt in unquenchable fire." Using exhortations like this, John proclaimed the Good News to the people.

*SAINT JOHN THE BAPTIST (FIRST CENTURY)*

✤ ✤ ✤

I long to hear you spoken, O Good News, and to proclaim your presence to all of creation. Yet I am no better than your disciple Thomas, needing to experience God's wonders directly, personally. So I pray, reveal to me your omnipresence, explain to me your immanence, that I might finally put aside my doubting and trust joyfully in your coming. Amen.

# DAY 20

*Adonai, my God,*
*you are the One I seek.*
*My soul thirsts for you,*
*my body longs for you*
*in this dry and weary land*
*where there is no water.*
*So I look to you in the sanctuary*
*to see your power and glory;*
*because your love is better than life,*
*my lips will glorify you.*

PSALM 63:1–3

# O God of Seeking!

Teach me to seek you,
    and when I seek you, show yourself to me;
        for I cannot seek you unless you teach me,
        or find you unless you show yourself to me.
Let me seek you by desiring you,
    and desire you by seeking you.
Let me find you by loving you,
    and love you when I find you.
I do not seek to understand so that I can believe,
    but I believe so that I may understand.
For this too I believe:
Unless I believe, I shall not understand.

*SAINT ANSELM OF CANTERBURY (1033–1109)*

✤ ✤ ✤

O God of Seeking, it seems I am always looking for the end instead of the way. I search for love instead of loving, for belief instead of believing, and I remain unmoved. But you are the Way, and the Way is all the heaven I need. I pray for your reassurance in this profession of my faith, that I might finally accept and rejoice in your living, life-giving, and eternal presence. Amen.

## DAY 21

*The grace of God has appeared, offering salvation to all. It trains us to reject godless ways and worldly desires, and to live temperately, justly and devoutly in this age as we await our blessed hope—the appearing of the glory of our great God and our Savior Jesus Christ.*

TITUS 2:11–13

# O God of Sustenance!

*A*h! Jesus, my heart's beloved, surely no spiritual plant can bear fruit unless it is drenched in the dew of your Spirit, unless it is nourished by the strength of your love....

By your grace make me flower like the lilies of the valley on the banks of flowing streams.

*SAINT GERTRUDE THE GREAT (1256–1302)*

✤ ✤ ✤

O God of Sustenance, why did you call me to this journey? It has consumed my very soul, until I feel that nothing of myself remains. As I begin this final week of Advent, I plead for spiritual nourishment. Revive my exhausted spirit and carry me forward, that I might make my way to Bethlehem at last to partake of the bread of your resurrection life. Amen.

*Like a stag, a doe, longing for streams of cool water,*
*my whole being longs for you, my God.*
*My soul aches with thirst for God, for a god that lives!*
*When can I go and see God face to face?*

PSALM 42:1–2

## *O God of Longing!*

With longing I gaze into the starlit sky,
   Into the sapphire of fathomless firmaments.
   There the pure heart leaps out to find You, O God,
   And yearns to be freed of the bonds of the flesh.

With great longing, I gaze upon you, my homeland.
   When will this, my exile, come to an end?
   O Jesus, such is the call of Your bride
   Who suffers agony in her thirst for You.

With longing, I gaze at the footprints of the saints
Who crossed this wilderness on their way....
They left me the example of their virtue and their counsels,
And they say to me,
　　"Patience, Sister, soon the fetters will break."

But my longing soul hears not these words.
Ardently; it yearns for its Lord and its God,
And it understands not human language,
Because it is enamored of Him alone.

My longing soul, wounded with love,
Forces its way through all created things
And unites itself with infinite eternity,
With the Lord whom my heart has espoused.

Allow my longing soul, O God,
To be drowned in Your Divine Three-fold Essence.
Fulfill my desires, for which I humbly beg You,
With a heart brimming with love's fire.

*SAINT FAUSTINA KOWALSKA (1905–1938)*

❖ ❖ ❖

O God of Longing, my soul is filled with great longings—for tranquillity, for love, for connectedness—and the greatest desire of my soul is to see you, to speak with you, to touch you, to be in your presence. Yet why do I not apprehend your face in the faces of my neighbors? Why do I not recognize your Spirit all around me? Dear God, in this final week of Advent, unveil for me the mystery of your immanence, that I might finally begin to comprehend the true meaning of your incarnation. Amen.

# DAY 23

*Do not remember the former things,*
*or consider the things of old.*
*I am about to do a new thing;*
*now it springs forth, do you not perceive it?*

ISAIAH 43:18–19

*The days are surely coming, says the LORD, when I will make a new covenant with the house of Israel and the house of Judah. It will not be like the covenant that I made with their ancestors when I took them by the hand to bring them out of the land of Egypt.... But this is the covenant that I will make with the house of Israel after those days, says the LORD: I will put my law within them, and I will write it on their hearts; and I will be their God, and they shall be my people.*

JEREMIAH 31:31–33

# O God of New Beginnings!

In the beginning
> there was the Word;
> the Word was in God's presence,
>> and the Word was God.
> The Word was present to God
>> from the beginning.
> Through the Word
>> all things came into being,
and apart from the Word
>> nothing came into being
>> that has come into being.
In the Word was life,
>> and that life was humanity's light—
a Light that shines in the darkness,
>> a Light that the darkness has never overtaken.

SAINT JOHN THE EVANGELIST (FIRST CENTURY)

✤ ✤ ✤

O God of New Beginnings, I perceive your Spirit moving through creation, and I am terrified of the changes you are sending my way. Shall I flee, hide, or dispute your Word? As you spoke to your prophets, so speak to me, that I might comprehend what you are now creating and rejoice in this brand-new beginning. Amen.

## DAY 24

The Pharisees asked Jesus when the reign of God would come.

Jesus replied, "The reign of God doesn't come in a visible way. You can't say, 'See, here it is!' or 'There it is!' No—look: the reign of God is already in your midst."

LUKE 17:20–21

# O God Within!

And should by chance you do not know
    Where to find Me,
    Do not go here and there;
    But if you wish to find Me,
    *In yourself seek Me.*

    Soul, since you are My room,
    My house and dwelling,
    If at any time,
    Through your distracted ways
    I find the door tightly closed,

    Outside of yourself seek Me not,
    To find Me it will be
    Enough only to call Me,
    Then quickly will I come,
    *And in yourself seek Me.*

*SAINT TERESA OF ÁVILA (1515–1582)*

✤ ✤ ✤

"I am with you always, even until the end of the world!" you promised, but my restless soul casts about frantically, desperately, for some hint of your continued existence. O God Within, please comfort my seeking soul, that, sensing your Spirit, I might begin to trust in your promise. Help me rediscover the Divine inside myself, that I might abandon this exhausting hunt for external evidence once and for all. Enfold me with your loving presence, that I might never lose you nor forget where to find you. Amen.

# DAY 25

*Finally they said to him, "Who are you? Give us an answer to take back to those who sent us. What do you have to say for yourself?"*

*John said, "I am, as Isaiah prophesied, the voice of someone crying out in the wilderness, 'Make straight Our God's road!'"*

*The emissaries were members of the Pharisee sect. They questioned him further: "If you're not the Messiah or Elijah or the Prophet, then why are you baptizing people?"*

*John said, "I baptize with water because among you stands someone whom you don't recognize—the One who is to come after me— the strap of whose sandal I am not worthy even to untie."...*

*The next day, catching sight of Jesus approaching, John exclaimed, "Look, there's God's sacrificial lamb, who takes away the world's sin! This is the one I was talking about when I said, 'The one who comes after me ranks ahead of me, for this One existed before I did.' I didn't recognize him, but it was so that he would be revealed to Israel that I came baptizing with water."*

*John also gave this testimony: "I saw the Spirit descend from heaven like a dove, and she came to rest on him. I didn't recognize him, but the One who sent me to baptize with water told me, 'When you see the Spirit descend and rest on someone, that is the One who will baptize with the Holy Spirit.' Now I have seen for myself and have testified that this is the Only Begotten of God."*

JOHN 1:22–34

# O God of Prophecy!

My Lord, my Spouse, You have given Yourself to me partially; now may You give me Yourself more completely. You have revealed Yourself to me as through fissures in a rock; now may You give me that revelation more clearly. You have communicated by means of others, as if joking with me; now may You truly grant me a communication of Yourself by Yourself. In

Your visits, at times, it seems You are about to give me the jewel of possessing You; but when I become aware of this possession, I discover that I do not have it, for You hide this jewel as if You had given it jokingly. Now wholly surrender Yourself by giving Yourself entirely to all of me, that my entire soul may have complete possession of You.

Do not send me
Any more messengers,
They cannot tell me what I must hear.

SAINT JOHN OF THE CROSS (1542–1591)

❖ ❖ ❖

O God of Prophecy, I no longer trust those prophets—on television or radio, in newspapers or books, or even at seminaries or in pulpits—who profess to teach me who you are. Their words are glib, their messages meaningless, their prophecies inconsequential. The scriptures themselves are cryptic, the biblical prophets seem irrelevant, and the historical record is unsatisfying. Please send me no more oracles, but reveal yourself to me directly, that I might experience the Divine with my own senses, that I might befriend you personally, that I might learn from you all I need to know on my Advent journey. Become for me a burning bush or pillar of fire, and lead me to that happy reunion with you that I have craved since my birth. Amen.

# DAY 26

"Blessed are those whose hearts are clean:
they will see God."

MATTHEW 5:8


Jesus then said,
"You've become a believer
because you saw me.
Blessed are those who have not seen
and yet have believed."

JOHN 20:29

# O God of Blessings!

*O* lovely Infant Jesus, You will abide with me once more. O that I might prepare for You an agreeable dwelling place in my heart. Jesus, Almighty Savior, come to my aid! Dearest Jesus, wash me with the tears which my sins draw from Your sweet eyes. Bless me, hands of my infant Savior! Lips of my Jesus, open to me and say, 'Your sins are forgiven.' May Your love remain in my heart, dear Jesus!…Be born again in me. Bless me and give me simplicity of heart, humility and obedience.

*SAINT JOHN NEUMANN (1811–1860)*

✦ ✦ ✦

O God of Blessings, I pray for your threefold blessing: Bless me with the spirit of renovation, that I might prepare a dwelling place for you in my heart. Bless me with the spirit of repentance, that I might return to your presence. Bless me with the spirit of resurrection, that I might rejoice in the rebirth of your Spirit in my soul. Amen.

## DAY 27

*The LORD is the everlasting God,*
*the Creator of the ends of the earth.*
*He does not faint or grow weary;*
*his understanding is unsearchable.*
*He gives power to the faint,*
*and strengthens the powerless.*
*Even youths will faint and be weary,*
*and the young will fall exhausted;*
*but those who wait for the LORD*
*shall renew their strength,*
*they shall mount up with wings like eagles,*
*they shall run and not be weary,*
*they shall walk and not faint.*

ISAIAH 40:28–31

# O God of Resurrection!

*A*las! it is already late, I am overcome with sleep and my pen slips from my fingers. Let me sleep a little, O Jesus, while your Mother and Saint Joseph are preparing the room.

I will lie down to rest here, in the fresh night air. As soon as you come the splendour of your light will dazzle my eyes. Your angels will awaken me with sweet hymns of glory and peace and I shall run forward with joy to welcome you and to offer you my own poor gifts, my home, all the little I have. I will worship you and show you all my love, with the other shepherds who have joined me and with the angels of heaven, singing hymns of glory to your Sacred Heart. Come, I am longing for you.

*BLESSED POPE JOHN XXIII*

✢ ✢ ✢

I praise and thank you, O God of Resurrection, for restoring my strength and reviving my spirits throughout this long and wearying season. I have nothing to offer in return, only my hospitality for you who are Hospitality and my love for you who are Love. Accept these poor gifts, I pray, and come, abide with me. Amen.

# DAY 28

"The ruler will say to those on the right, 'Come, you blessed of my Abba God! Inherit the kindom prepared for you from the creation of the world! For I was hungry and you fed me; I was thirsty and you gave me drink. I was a stranger and you welcomed me; naked and you clothed me. I was ill and you comforted me; in prison and you came to visit me.' Then these just will ask, 'When did we see you hungry and feed you, or see you thirsty and give you drink? When did we see you as a stranger and invite you in, or clothe you in your nakedness? When did we see you ill or in prison and come to visit you?' The ruler will answer them, 'The truth is, every time you did this for the least of my sisters or brothers, you did it for me.'"

MATTHEW 25:34–40

# O God of the Poor!

All mayors of towns and lords of castles and villages should be obliged each year on the Nativity of our Lord to see that their people scatter wheat and other grain on the roads outside towns and villages, so that our sisters the larks and other birds may have food on such a solemn festival. And in reverence for the Son of God, Who with the most blessed Virgin Mary rested in a manger that night between an ox and an ass, anyone who owns an ox or an ass should be obliged to give them the choicest of fodder on Christmas Eve. And on Christmas Day the rich should give an abundance of good things to all the poor.

*SAINT FRANCIS OF ASSISI (1181–1226)*

✤ ✤ ✤

It's easy for me to pray for the sick, to prepare meals for a food pantry or bring clothes to a shelter, even to serve meals in a soup kitchen. You call me blessed for these simple efforts, yet I sacrifice nothing, merely a little time cornered in between mailing Christmas packages and picking up the Christmas tree. Is that all you expect from a soul named "blessed"? I expect more from myself—at least the capacity to leaven these acts with a little love. O God of the Poor, I pray that your coming into the world on this night will bring a personal miracle, the re-creation of my soul in your blessed image and the incarnation of your Love in my heart. Amen.

## PART II
~~~~~~

# READINGS *for the* TWELVE DAYS *of* CHRISTMAS

*Praise Our God from the earth,*
*you sea creatures and ocean depths,*
*lightning and hail, snow and mist,*
*and storm winds that fulfill God's word,*
*mountains and all hills,*
*fruit trees and all cedars,*
*wild animals and all cattle,*
*small animals and flying birds,*
*rulers of the earth, leaders of all nations,*
*all the judges in the world,*
*young men and young women,*
*old people and children—*
*let them praise the Name of Our God*
*whose Name alone is exalted,*
*whose majesty transcends heaven and earth,*
*and who has raised up a Horn for God's people*

*to the praise of the faithful,*
*the children of Israel, the people dear to God!*
*Alleluia!*

PSALM 148:7–14

## *O Immanuel!*

*M*y soul has longed for you all night, O eternal wisdom! and in the early morning I turn to you from the depths of my heart. May your holy presence remove all dangers from my soul and body. May your many graces fill the inmost recesses of my heart, and inflame it with your divine love.

O most sweet Jesus! turn your face toward me, for this morning with all the powers of my soul I fly to you and greet you, entreating that the thousand times a thousand angels who minister to you may praise you on my behalf, and that the thousand times ten thousand blessed spirits who surround your throne may glorify you today. May all that is beautiful and lovable in created beings praise you for me, and may all creation bless your holy name, our help and protection in time and in eternity.

*BLESSED HENRY SUSO (C. 1295–1366)*

✣ ✣ ✣

With cries of joy I greet your birth, O Immanuel! All glory, praise, and honor to you!

Thanks be to the God of Creation for the gift of your Incarnation. Amen.

# DAY 2

There were shepherds in the area living in the fields and keeping nightwatch by turns over their flock. The angel of God appeared to them, and the glory of God shone around them; they were very much afraid.

The angel said to them, "You have nothing to fear! I come to proclaim good news to you—news of a great joy to be shared by the whole people. Today in David's city, a savior—the Messiah—has been born to you. Let this be a sign to you: you'll find an infant wrapped in a simple cloth, lying in a manger."

Suddenly, there was a multitude of the heavenly host with the angel, praising God and saying,

"Glory to God in high heaven!
And on earth, peace to those on whom God's favor rests."

When the angels had returned to heaven, the shepherds said to one another, "Let's go straight to Bethlehem and see this event that God has made known to us." They hurried and *found Mary and Joseph, and the baby lying in the manger; once they saw this, they reported what they had been told concerning the child.*

LUKE 2:8–17

## O Child of Divinity!

*O*ne thing is necessary: to be near Jesus. You know well that at the birth of Our Lord the shepherds heard the angelic and divine chants of the heavenly spirits. The Scriptures say so. But they do not say that His Virgin Mother and St. Joseph, who were nearer to the Child, heard the voices of the angels or saw those miracles of splendor. On the contrary, they heard the Child weeping and saw by the light of a poor lantern the eyes of the Divine Child all bathed in tears, in sighs and shivering with cold. Now I ask you: Would you not have preferred to have been in the dark stable, filled with the cries of the little Child, rather than to have been with the shepherds, besides yourself with joy over those sweet melodies from heaven and the beauties of this wonderful splendor?

*SAINT PADRE PIO (1887–1968)*

❖ ❖ ❖

O Child of Divinity, why do I seek God in the spectacular—in a glorious sunrise, a sweet melody, a sacred ceremony, an inspired prayer? Teach me, rather, to seek the Divine in the ordinary—in my grandmother's hands or my brother's face, in my child's laughter or my own baby's wail—so that I might, finally, come to perceive God in all things and to be with God as God is always with me. Amen.

# DAY 3

*But you, O Bethlehem of Ephrathah,*
*who are one of the little clans of Judah,*
*from you shall come forth for me*
*one who is to rule in Israel,*
*whose origin is from of old,*
*from ancient of days.*

MICAH 5:2

## O Baby of Bethlehem!

Let us pass over to Bethlehem and see this great vision, this Word that is made. It is necessary that we pass over everything that is visible, everything that is changeable, everything that can vary this way and that, everything that can know alteration, in order that we may take our heart from everything vain and voluptuous and all that could feed it with evil pleasures. May there only be a taste for that bread which comes down from heaven and gives life to the world. Thus our mind might be made a house of bread, that is a Bethlehem. Then we will see there this Word which is made. There he will show himself to us, this fire which Moses desired to see....

But you who now build a Bethlehem in your own soul and pass over the lusts of the world, worldly riches and deceptive honors, you will then see Jesus, little and humble, you yourselves little and humble as you look upon his sweet face. And so you will hear his most sweet voice: "Come, blessed of my Father. Receive the kingdom, which has been prepared from the beginning of the world." Then you will enter into that kingdom and you will see Jesus, sweet and lovable.... There truly is Bethlehem, truly the house of bread, which will satisfy our desire for the good when our youth will be renewed as the eagles. Let us pass over to this Bethlehem and there see this Word which today is made. Let us pass over, let us pass over now in hope and desire, in love and affection.

SAINT AELRED OF RIEVAULX (1110–1167)

✣ ✣ ✣

O Baby of Bethlehem, with so many new toys to play with, so many gifts to exchange, so many after-Christmas sales to attend, I might now easily lose sight of you hidden in a feeding trough in a broken-down stable in some obscure desert village. Send me some messenger, some missive—a late greeting card, perhaps, or a stranger in need of some holiday cheer—so that I might pass over your post-birthday rush, putting aside the presents that shine so blindingly or the activities that call so insistently, and continue on my journey to Bethlehem. Please illuminate my way with your true light, and help me to discern the important from the urgent and thus to rush quickly into your presence. Amen.

# DAY 4

*Thus says the LORD:*
*A voice is heard in Ramah,*
*lamentation and bitter weeping.*
*Rachel is weeping for her children;*
*she refuses to be comforted for her children,*
*because they are no more.*
*Thus says the LORD:*
*Keep your voice from weeping,*
*and your eyes from tears;*
*for there is a reward for your work,*
*says the LORD:*
*they shall come back from the land of the enemy;*
*there is hope for your future,*
*says the LORD:*
*your children shall come back to their own country.*

JEREMIAH 31:15–17

# O Child of the Hour!

*In* this brilliant night which illuminates the joy of the Holy Trinity, Jesus, the gentle little Child of the hour…made me strong and brave. He armed me with his weapons and, since that blessed night, I have not been defeated in any battle. To the contrary, I went from one victory to the next, to begin, more or less, "an invincible quest."

*SAINT THÉRÈSE OF LISIEUX (1873–1897)*

✤ ✤ ✤

O Child of the Hour, the light of glory shines upon you, and all of creation is attentive to your presence. But as you always concerned yourself with the needs of others, so redirect my attention to the children around me who today do not have all that they need. They are your incarnation in today's world, and as I love them, so I show my love for you. Help me find them, feed them, clothe them, shelter them, and, especially, love them, with all my being, just as you love me. Amen.

# DAY 5

*Then I saw new heavens and a new earth. The former heavens and the former earth had passed away, and the sea existed no longer. I also saw a new Jerusalem, the holy city, coming down out of heaven from God, beautiful as a bride and groom on their wedding day.*

*And I heard a loud voice calling from the throne, "Look! God's Tabernacle is among humankind! God will live with them; they will be God's people, and God will be fully present among them. The Most High will wipe away every tear from their eyes. And death, mourning, crying and pain will be no more, for the old order has fallen."*

*The One who sat on the throne said, "Look! I'm making everything new!"*

REVELATION 21:1–5

# O Child of God!

The son of man, in assuming our flesh, certainly did not come to us for any light reason, but for our very great benefit. For he, as it were, traded with us by assuming a living body and deigning to be born of the Virgin so that we may participate in his divinity. And so he became man in order to make man divine.

*SAINT THOMAS AQUINAS (1226–1274)*

❖ ❖ ❖

Grant me your blessing, O Child of God, for I too am Abba's child. As you share in my humanity, I share in your divinity. Inscribe this knowledge in my soul, I pray, that I might never forsake my birthright. Inspire me so to live that my every word and deed become revelations of the Divine, moments when the kindom of God can break forth into the world. Amen.

# DAY 6

Beloved,
let us love one another
because love is of God;
everyone who loves is begotten of God
and has knowledge of God.
Those who do not love have known nothing of God,
for God is love....
No one has ever seen God.
Yet if we love one another,
God dwells in us,
and God's love is brought to perfection in us....
God is love,
and those who abide in love
abide in God,
and God in them.

1 JOHN 4:7–16

# O Child of Love!

*The* Blessed Virgin alone conceived Christ in her womb, yet all the elect carry him in the devotion of their hearts. Happy and most blessed the woman who bore him for nine months in her womb. Happy also we, if we diligently strive to bear him in our thoughts. It was indeed wondrous that Christ was conceived in a womb, but it is no less striking that he be borne in the prison of the heart.

Consider, dearly beloved, what a dignity is ours, and what a likeness there is between us and Mary. Mary conceived Christ in her womb, and we bear him about in our heart. Mary fed Christ when she gave milk from her breasts to his tender lips, and we feed him with the varied delights of our good works.

*SAINT PETER DAMIAN (1007–1072)*

✤ ✤ ✤

O Child of Love, born of God's great love for humanity, you have come into the world to demonstrate the meaning of love, and your life was a model of love in action. Open my heart to your example, and help me so to live that my life becomes a reflection of your love and a revelation of God's love to all. Amen.

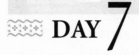

# DAY 7

*For a child has been born for us,*
*a son given to us;*
*authority rests upon his shoulders;*
*and he is named*
*Wonderful Counselor, Mighty God,*
*Everlasting Father, Prince of Peace.*
*His authority shall grow continually,*
*and there shall be endless peace*
*for the throne of David and his kingdom.*
*He will establish and uphold it*
*with justice and with righteousness*
*from this time onward and forevermore.*

ISAIAH 9:6–7

# O Child of Nazareth!

*C*hristmastime shows us how small God made himself. Go to the crib and see how small he became, how he lived that total surrender to the full.

We must learn to be that child in complete surrender and trust and joy.

See the joy of the child Jesus and the joy of Christmas! Never be moody, never let anything take away that joy. Christmas shows us how much heaven appreciates humility, surrender, poverty, because God himself, who made you and me, became so small, so poor, so humble.

*MOTHER TERESA OF CALCUTTA (1910–1997)*

✣ ✣ ✣

O Child of Nazareth, you have taught me that Christmas is not just for the children around me but also for the child hidden so deeply within me. Touch my heart with your newly born wonder, that I might experience the events of this season from a child's innocent and simple perspective—and that I might from this moment forward savor all of my life with the awe, joy, and love that are your true gifts to all children. Amen.

## DAY 8

*Your attitude must be the same as that of Christ Jesus:*
*Christ, though in the image of God,*
*didn't deem equality with God*
*something to be clung to—*
*but instead became completely empty*
*and took on the image of oppressed humankind:*
*born into the human condition,*
*found in the likeness of a human being.*

PHILIPPIANS 2:5–7

# O Babe of the Manger!

*R*ejoice and be glad that so great and good a Lord, on coming into the Virgin's womb willed to appear despised, needy
and poor in this world, so that men who were in dire poverty and
suffering great need of heavenly food might be made rich in him.

*SAINT CLARE OF ASSISI (1193–1253)*

✤ ✤ ✤

Laid in an animal's feeding trough, you knew the
direst needs of the human condition from the
very moment of your birth. Yet your presence transformed
that manger in Bethlehem into a splendid cradle, those
swaddling rags into splendid robes, and that smelly cave
into a gilded hall. O Babe of the Manger, help me to appreciate all that I have and to rejoice in the abundance
with which God has blessed my life. And in those moments when I find myself oppressed by need, or wishing
for even more than I have, startle my soul with your transforming presence, that I might apprehend all around me
the heavenly bounty my loving God has already provided.
Amen.

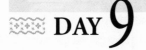

## DAY 9

> ...*God highly exalted Christ*
> *and gave to Jesus the name above every other name,*
> *so that at the name of Jesus every knee must bend*
> *in the heavens, on the earth and under the earth,*
> *and every tongue proclaim to the glory of God:*
> *Jesus Christ reigns supreme!*
>
> PHILIPPIANS 2:9–11

# O Infant so Sweet!

*J*esus is honey in the mouth, music in the ear and a shout of joy in the heart.

*SAINT BERNARD OF CLAIRVAUX (C. 1090–1153)*

✣ ✣ ✣

O Infant so Sweet, as any newborn, yours was the scent of ambrosial perfume, the cry of heavenly music, the likeness of an angel, the touch of gossamer. No wonder angels came to announce you, shepherds to greet you, and Magi to praise you. So too I return to your manger, to celebrate again your miraculous presence. Amen.

# DAY 10

Jesus said, "If you want to be perfect, go and sell what you own and give the money to poor people, and you will have treasure in heaven. Then come and follow me."…

Jesus said to the disciples, "The truth is, it is difficult for a rich person to enter the kindom of heaven. I'll say it again—it is easier for a camel to pass through the Needle's Eye gate than for the wealthy to enter the kindom of heaven."

When the disciples heard this, they were astonished. "Then who can be saved?" they said.

Jesus looked at them and said, "For mortals it is impossible, but for God everything is possible."

Then Peter spoke: "We have left everything and followed you. What then will there be for us?"

Jesus said, "…everyone who has left home, sisters, brothers, mother, father, children or land for my sake will be repaid a hundredfold, and will also inherit eternal life."

MATTHEW 19:21–29

# O Child of Poverty!

*P*overty is true riches. So precious is poverty that God's Only-Begotten Son came on earth in search of it. In heaven he had superabundance of all goods. Nothing was lacking there but poverty.

SAINT ANTHONY OF PADUA (1195–1231)

✤ ✤ ✤

O Child of Poverty, I am so possessive, so at-tached, and so selfish, even of those gifts I have just received. But you have promised me heaven and better treasures than I can ever imagine. Strengthen my faith in what is to come, that I might free myself from my fearful acquisitiveness and begin to share my abundance with those in need, bringing a little bit of heaven to the here and now. Amen.

# DAY 11

*And the Word became flesh*
*and stayed for a little while among us;*
*we saw the Word's glory—*
*the favor and position a parent gives an only child—*
*filled with grace,*
*filled with truth....*
*Of this One's fullness*
*we've all had a share—*
*gift on top of gift.*
*For while the Law was given through Moses,*
*the Gift—and the Truth—came through Jesus Christ.*
*No one has ever seen God;*
*it is the Only Begotten,*
*ever at Abba's side,*
*who has revealed God to us.*

JOHN 1:14, 16–18

# O Child of the Word!

*T*he first Adam, as scripture says, "became a living soul," but the last Adam has become a life-giving spirit. That is, the natural comes first, not the spiritual; after that comes the spiritual. The first, being from the earth, is earthly by nature; the second is from heaven. As this earthly one was, so are we of the earth; and as the One from heaven is, so are we in heaven. And we, who have been modeled on the earthly, likewise will be modeled on the One from heaven.

*SAINT PAUL THE APOSTLE (FIRST CENTURY)*

❖ ❖ ❖

Each day the world is created anew, and every moment is a new incarnation, a new infusion of the Divine. O Child of the Word, open my heart to your abiding presence, that I might not only recognize but rejoice in the ongoing incarnation of the Word as I proceed through this blessed day. Amen.

## ❧❧ DAY 12 ❧❧❧❧❧❧❧❧❧❧❧

*After Jesus' birth—which happened in Bethlehem of Judea,
during the reign of Herod—astrologers from the East arrived
in Jerusalem and asked, "Where is the newborn ruler of the
Jews? We observed his star at its rising, and have come to pay
homage." At this news Herod became greatly disturbed, as did
all of Jerusalem. Summoning all the chief priests and religious
scholars of the people, he asked them where the Messiah was to
be born.*

*"In Bethlehem of Judea," they informed him....*

*Herod called the astrologers aside and found out from them
the exact time of the star's appearance. Then he sent them to
Bethlehem....*

*After their audience with the ruler, they set out. The star
which they had observed at its rising went ahead of them until
it came to a standstill over the place where the child lay. They
were overjoyed at seeing the star and, upon entering the house,*

*found the child with Mary, his mother. They prostrated them-*
*selves and paid homage. Then they opened their coffers and*
*presented the child with gifts of gold, frankincense and myrrh.*

## *O Holy Infant!*

His light shone out over the east;
> Persia was enlightened by the star:
> *His* Epiphany gave good tidings to her and invited her,
> "He is come for the sacrifice that brings joy to all."

The star of light hasted and came and dawned
through the darkness, and summoned them
that the peoples should come and exult
in the great Light that has come down to earth.

One envoy from among the stars
the firmament sent to proclaim to them,
to the sons of Persia, that they might make ready
to meet the King and to worship Him.

Great Assyria when she perceived *it*
called to the Magi and said to them,
"Take gifts and go, honour Him
the great King Who in Judea has dawned."

The princes of Persia, exulting,
carried gifts from their region;
and they brought to the Son of the Virgin
gold and myrrh and frankincense.

They entered and found Him as a child
as he dwelt in the house of the lowly woman;
and they drew near and worshipped with gladness,
and brought near before Him their treasures....

Let the Church sing with rejoicing,
"Glory in the Birth of the Highest,
by Whom the world above and the world below are illumined!"
Blessed *be* He in Whose Birth all are made glad!

SAINT EPHREM THE SYRIAN (D. 373)

✤ ✤ ✤

Here I am, O Holy Infant. As the Magi carried the good news of your birth to the wide world, so anoint me as your messenger, that I too might bear the news of your immanence to a people in need of rejoicing, both today and throughout the coming year. Amen.

PART III

~~~~~~

A FORMAT for
NIGHTLY PRAYER
and READING

# Format for Nightly Prayer and Reading

The purpose of presenting these two optional formats for nightly readings and prayer is to offer a way to use the material in this book as an opportunity for group or individual prayer. Of course, there are other ways in which to use this material, for example, as a vehicle for meditation or as promptings for completing a prayer journal.

# FORMAT 1

## OPENING PRAYER

The observance begins with these words:

*God, come to my assistance.*
*Lord, make haste to help me.*

followed by:

*Glory to the Father, and to the Son,*
*and to the Holy Spirit, as it was in the beginning,*
*is now, and will be, for ever. Amen. Alleluia!*

## EXAMINATION OF CONSCIENCE

If this observance is being prayed individually, an examination of conscience may be included. Here is a short examination of conscience; you may, of course, use your own preferred method.

1. Place yourself in a quiet frame of mind.
2. Review your life since your last confession.
3. Reflect on the Ten Commandments and any sins against these commandments.
4. Reflect on the words of the gospel, especially Jesus' commandment to love your neighbor as yourself.
5. Ask yourself these questions: How have I been unkind in thoughts, words, and actions? Am I refusing to forgive anyone? Do I despise any group or person? Am I a prisoner of fear, anxiety, worry, guilt, inferiority, or hatred of myself?

## PENITENTIAL RITE (OPTIONAL)

If a group of people are praying in unison, a penitential rite from the Roman Missal may be used:

*Presider:* Lord Jesus, you came to call all people to yourself: Lord, have mercy.

*All:* Lord, have mercy.

*Presider:* Lord Jesus, you come to us in word and prayer: Christ, have mercy.

*All:* Christ, have mercy.

*Presider:* Lord Jesus, you will appear in glory with all your saints: Lord, have mercy.

*All:* Lord, have mercy.

*Presider:* May almighty God have mercy on us, forgive us our sins, and bring us to life everlasting.

*All:* Amen.

# HYMN: O COME, O COME, EMMANUEL

A hymn is now sung or recited. This Advent hymn is a paraphrase of the "Great O" Antiphons written in the twelfth century and translated by John Mason Neale in 1852.

O come, O come, Emmanuel,
And ransom captive Israel;
That mourns in lonely exile here,
Until the Son of God appear.

*Refrain:*     Rejoice! Rejoice!
          O Israel! To thee shall come, Emmanuel!

O come, thou wisdom, from on high,
And order all things far and nigh;
To us the path of knowledge show,
And teach us in her ways to go.

*Refrain*

O come, O come, thou Lord of might,
Who to thy tribes on Sinai's height
In ancient times did give the law,
In cloud, and majesty, and awe.

*Refrain*

O come, thou rod of Jesse's stem,
From ev'ry foe deliver them
That trust thy mighty power to save,
And give them vict'ry o'er the grave.

*Refrain*

O come, thou key of David, come,
And open wide our heav'nly home,
Make safe the way that leads on high,
That we no more have cause to sigh.

*Refrain*

O come, thou Dayspring from on high,
And cheer us by thy drawing nigh;
Disperse the gloomy clouds of night
And death's dark shadow put to flight.

*Refrain*

O come, Desire of nations, bind
In one the hearts of all mankind;
Bid every strife and quarrel cease
And fill the world with heaven's peace.

*Refrain*

## PSALM 27:7–14—GOD STANDS BY US IN DANGERS

Hear, O LORD, when I cry aloud,
    be gracious to me and answer me!
"Come," my heart says, "seek his face!"
    Your face, LORD, do I seek.
    Do not hide your face from me.

Do not turn your servant away in anger,
    you who have been my help.
Do not cast me off, do not forsake me,
    O God of my salvation!
If my father and mother forsake me,
    the LORD will take me up.

Teach me your way, O LORD,
  and lead me on a level path
  because of my enemies.
Do not give me up to the will of my adversaries,
  for false witnesses have risen against me,
  and they are breathing out violence.

I believe that I shall see the goodness of the LORD
  in the land of the living.
Wait for the LORD;
  be strong, and let your heart take courage;
  wait for the LORD!

## RESPONSE

I long to see your face, O Lord. You are my light and my help. Do not turn away from me.

## SCRIPTURE READING

Read silently or have a presider proclaim the Scripture of the day that is selected.

## RESPONSE

Come and set us free, Lord God of power and might. Let your face shine on us and we will be saved.

*Glory be to the Father, and to the Son,
and to the Holy Spirit, as it was in the beginning,
is now, and will be for ever. Amen.*

## SECOND READING

Read the excerpt from the saint for the day selected.

## CANTICLE OF SIMEON

Lord, now you let your servant go in peace;
your word has been fulfilled:
my own eyes have seen the salvation
which you have prepared in the sight of every people:
a light to reveal you to the nations
and the glory of your people Israel.
Glory to the Father, and to the Son, and to the Holy Spirit,
as it was in the beginning, is now, and will be for ever. Amen.

## PRAYER

Say the prayer that follows the selected excerpt from that day's saint.

## BLESSING

May the Lord grant us a restful night and a peaceful death. Amen.

## MARIAN ANTIPHON

Loving mother of the Redeemer,
gate of heaven, star of the sea,
assist your people who have fallen yet strive to rise again.
To the wonderment of nature you bore your Creator,
yet remained a virgin after as before.
You who received Gabriel's joyful greeting,
have pity on us poor sinners.

## OPENING PRAYER

The observance begins with these words:

> *God, come to my assistance.*
> *Lord, make haste to help me.*

followed by:

> *Glory to the Father, and to the Son,*
> *and to the Holy Spirit, as it was in the beginning,*
> *is now, and will be, for ever. Amen. Alleluia!*

## EXAMINATION OF CONSCIENCE

If this observance is being prayed individually, an examination of conscience may be included. Here is a short examination of conscience; you may, of course, use your own preferred method.

1. Place yourself in a quiet frame of mind.
2. Review your life since your last confession.
3. Reflect on the Ten Commandments and any sins against these commandments.
4. Reflect on the words of the gospel, especially Jesus' commandment to love your neighbor as yourself.
5. Ask yourself these questions: How have I been unkind in thoughts, words, and actions? Am I refusing to forgive anyone? Do I despise any group or person? Am I a prisoner of fear, anxiety, worry, guilt, inferiority, or hatred of myself?

## PENITENTIAL RITE (OPTIONAL)

If a group of people are praying in unison, a penitential rite from the Roman Missal may be used:

*All:*     I confess to almighty God,
       and to you, my brothers and sisters,
       that I have sinned through my own fault
       in my thoughts and in my words,
       in what I have done,
       and in what I have failed to do;
       and I ask blessed Mary, ever virgin,
       all the angels and saints,
       and you, my brothers and sisters,
       to pray for me to the Lord our God.

*Presider:*  May almighty God have mercy on us,
       forgive us our sins,
       and bring us to life everlasting.

*All:*     Amen.

## HYMN: BEHOLD, A ROSE

A hymn is now sung or recited. This traditional hymn was composed in German in the fifteenth century. It is sung to the melody of the familiar "Lo, A Rose E're Blooming."

Behold, a rose of Judah
From tender branch has sprung,
From Jesse's lineage coming,
As men of old have sung.
It came a flower bright
Amid the cold of winter,
When half spent was the night.

Isaiah has foretold it
In words of promise sure,
And Mary's arms enfolt it,
A virgin meek and pure.
Through God's eternal will
She bore for men a savior
At midnight calm and still.

## PSALM 40:1–8—THANKSGIVING FOR DELIVERANCE

I waited patiently for the LORD;
    he inclined to me and heard my cry.
He drew me up from the desolate pit,
    out of the miry bog,
and set my feet upon a rock,
    making my steps secure.
He put a new song in my mouth,
    a song of praise to our God.

Many will see and fear,
and put their trust in the LORD.

Happy are those who make
the LORD their trust,
who do not turn to the proud,
to those who go astray after false gods.
You have multiplied, O LORD, my God,
your wondrous deeds and your thoughts toward us;
none can compare with you.
Were I to proclaim and tell of them,
they would be more than can be counted.

Sacrifice and offering you do not desire,
but you have given me an open ear.
Burnt offering and sin offering
you have not required.
Then I said, "Here I am;
in the scroll of the book it is written of me.
I delight to do your will, O my God;
your law is within my heart."

## RESPONSE

May all who seek after you be glad in the LORD; may those who find your salvation say with continuous praise, "Great is the LORD!"

## SCRIPTURE READING

Read silently or have a presider proclaim the Scripture of the day that is selected.

## RESPONSE

Lord, you who were made obedient unto death, teach us to always do the Father's will, so that, sanctified by the holy obedience that joins us to your sacrifice, we can count on your immense love in times of sorrow.

> *Glory be to the Father, and to the Son,*
> *and to the Holy Spirit, as it was in the beginning,*
> *is now, and will be for ever. Amen.*

## SECOND READING

Read silently or have a presider read the words of the saint for the day selected.

## CANTICLE OF SIMEON

Lord, now you let your servant go in peace;
your word has been fulfilled:
my own eyes have seen the salvation
which you have prepared in the sight of every people:
a light to reveal you to the nations
and the glory of your people Israel.
Glory to the Father, and to the Son,
    and to the Holy Spirit,
as it was in the beginning, is now,
    and will be for ever. Amen.

## PRAYER

Recite the prayer that follows the excerpt from the saint for the day selected.

## BLESSING

Lord, give our bodies restful sleep and let the work we have done today bear fruit in eternal life. Watch over us as we rest in your peace. Amen.

## MARIAN ANTIPHON

Hail, holy Queen, mother of mercy,
our life, our sweetness, and our hope.
To you do we cry,
poor banished children of Eve.
To you do we send up our sighs,
mourning and weeping in this vale of tears.
Turn then, most gracious advocate,
your eyes of mercy toward us,
and after this exile
show to us the blessed fruit of your womb, Jesus.
O clement, O loving,
O sweet Virgin Mary.

# $\mathcal{S}$ources and $\mathcal{A}$cknowledgments

I THANK JOHN CLEARY and his colleagues at Liguori Publications for their loving care in helping to bring this work to fruition. My special thanks go to Rayner W. Hesse, Jr., for his invaluable assistance and, most of all, his hearty support of all that I am.

Every effort has been made to locate and secure permission for the inclusion of all copyrighted material in this book. If any such acknowledgments have been inadvertently omitted, the publisher would appreciate receiving full information so that proper credit may be given in future editions.

In order of appearance:

Saint Anselm of Canterbury from *The Life of St. Anselm* by Eadmer. Oxford: Oxford University Press, 1972.

Saint Julian of Norwich from "The Thirteenth Showing" in chapter 32 of *The Revelation of Divine Love in Sixteen Showings Made to Dame Julian of Norwich*, trans. with a new introduction by M. L. del Mastro. Kent, Great Britain: Burns & Oates, 1994.

Saint Alphonsus Liguori from *Meditations on the Incarnation* in *The Way of Saint Alphonsus Liguori: Selected Writings on the Spiritual Life*, comp. Barry Ulanov. Liguori, Mo.: Liguori/Triumph, 1999.

Saint Frances Xavier Cabrini from *In Weakness, Strength: The Life and Missionary Activity of Saint Frances Xavier Cabrini* by Segundo Galilea. New York: Missionary Sisters of the Sacred Heart of Jesus, 1996.

The English translation of Saint Ambrose of Milan's Commentary on Luke from *The Liturgy of the Hours*. Copyright 1974, International Committee on English in the Liturgy, Inc. All rights reserved.

Saint Catherine of Siena from *The Communion of Saints: Prayers of the Famous*, ed. Horton Davies. Grand Rapids: William B. Eerdmans, 1990.

Saint Dimitrii of Rostov from *The Orthodox Way* by Bishop Kallistos Ware. Crestwood, N.Y.: St. Vladimir's Seminary Press, 1995. Reprinted by permission of St. Vladimir's Seminary Press, 575 Scarsdale Road, Crestwood, NY 10707.

Saint Hildegard of Bingen from *Collected Plays* by Charles Williams. New York: Oxford University Press, 1963.

Saint Nicholas of Myra from *The Golden Legend of Jacobus de Voragine* by Jacob of Voragine. New York: Longmans, Green & Co., 1941.

Blessed Elizabeth of the Trinity from *Sister Elizabeth of the Trinity: Spiritual Writings*. New York: P. J. Kennedy & Sons, 1962.

Saint Leo the Great from *Saints at Prayer*, comp. and ed. Raymond E. F. Larssen. New York: Coward-McCann, 1942. Public domain.

The Immaculate Conception, as revealed to Saint Birgitta of Sweden, from *The Revelations of Saint Bridget* (*Liber celestis*, vi., c. 55) as found in *Revelations of St. Bridget on the Life and Passion of Our Lord and the Life of His Blessed Mother.* Rockford, Ill.: TAN Books, 1984.

Saint Katharine Drexel from *Reflections on Life in the Vine.* (Sisters of the Blessed Sacrament, 1982), p. 13.

Saint Bede from *The Venerable Bede,* ed. Benedicta Ward, S.L.G. Harrisburg, Pa.: Morehouse Publishing, 1990.

Our Lady of Guadalupe, as told to Blessed Juan Diego, as found in *God-Sent: A History of the Accredited Apparitions of Mary,* by Roy Abraham Varghese. New York: The Crossroad Publishing Co., 2000, p. 92.

Saint Patrick (attributed) from St. Patrick's Breastplate in *The Confession of Saint Patrick and Letter to Coroticus,* trans. by John Skinner. New York: Image Books/Doubleday, 1998.

Saint Anselm of Canterbury from *Breakfast with the Saints: 120 Readings from Great Christians,* selected by LaVonne Neff, © 1996 by Servant Publications. Published by Servant Publications (www.servantpub .com), P.O. Box 8617, Ann Arbor, MI 48107. Used with permission.

Saint Gertrude the Great from *Breakfast with the Saints: 120 Readings from Great Christians,* selected by LaVonne Neff, © 1996 by Servant Publications. Published by Servant Publications (www.servantpub .com), P.O. Box 8617, Ann Arbor, MI 48107. Used with permission.

Saint Faustina Kowalska from 1934 entry in *Diary of Sister M. Faustina Kowalska* by Saint Sister Mary Faustina Kowalska. Stockbridge, Mass.: Marian Press, 1990. Copyright 1987 Congregation of Marians of the Immaculate Conception, Stockbridge, MA 01263. All rights reserved. Used with permission.

Saint Teresa of Ávila, *Poetry* 8, from *Teresa of Avila: An Introduction to Her Life and Writings* by Tessa Bielecki. New York: The Crossroad Publishing Co., 1994.

Saint John of the Cross from *The Collected Works of St. John of the Cross,* translated by Kieran Kavanaugh and Otilio Rodriguez. Copyright 1979, 1991 by Washington Province of Discalced Carmelites, ICS Publications, 2131 Lincoln Road, N.E., Washington, DC 20002-1199, U.S.A.

Saint John Neumann from *Saint John N. Neumann's Favorite Prayers: Taken from His Diary.* Saint John Neumann Shrine, 1019 North 5th St., Philadelphia, PA 19123.

Blessed Pope John XXIII, December 24, 1902, entry from *Journal of a Soul* by Pope John XXIII, trans. Dorothy White. New York: McGraw-Hill, 1964.

Saint Francis of Assisi, *Mirror of Perfection,* as found in *St. Francis of Assisi: Writings and Early Biographies* 3rd rev. ed., ed. Marion A. Habig. Chicago: Franciscan Herald Press, 1973.

Blessed Henry Suso from *Breakfast with the Saints: 120 Readings from Great Christians,* selected by LaVonne Neff, © 1996 by Servant Publications. Published by Servant Publications (www.servantpub .com), P.O. Box 8617, Ann Arbor, MI 48107. Used with permission.

Saint Padre Pio from *Padre Pio Counsels,* ed. P. Alessio Parente. The National Centre for Padre Pio, Inc., 2213 Old Route 100, Barto, PA 19504.

Saint Aelred of Rievaulx, *Sermon Three for the Nativity of the Lord* (8–19) from *Liturgical Sermons* I, tr. Theodore Berkeley and M. Basil Pennington, Cistercian Fathers 55. Kalamazoo, Mich.: Cistercian Publications, 2000.

Saint Thérèse of Lisieux, Manuscript A, folio 45, verso, from *The Complete Works of Thérèse of Lisieux.* CERF-DDB, 1992; as found in Constant Tonnelier, *15 Days of Prayer with Saint Thérèse of Lisieux,* trans. by Victoria Hébert and Denis Sabourin. Liguori, Mo.: Liguori Publications, 1999.

Saint Thomas Aquinas, *On the Articles of Faith and the Sacraments of the Church* article 3, as found in *An Aquinas Reader,* ed. by Mary T. Clark. New York: Fordham University Press, 2000, p. 394.

Saint Peter Damian from *St. Peter Damian: His Teaching on the Spiritual Life* by Owen J. Blum, O.F.M. Washington, D.C.: The Catholic University of America Press, 1947.

Mother Teresa of Calcutta from *Thirsting for God: A Yearbook of Prayers, Meditations, and Anecdotes,* compiled by Fr. Angelo Scolozzi, M.C. III.O. Copyright 1999 by Servant Publications (www.servantpub .com), P.O. Box 8617, Ann Arbor, MI 48107. Used with permission.

Saint Clare of Assisi from *The Legend and Writings of Saint Clare of Assisi.* St. Bonaventure, N.Y.: The Franciscan Institute, 1953.

Excerpts from *Bernard of Clairvaux: Selected Works,* translated and foreword by G. R. Evans, from The Classics of Western Spirituality, copyright 1987 by Gillian R. Evans, Paulist Press, Inc. New York/Mahwah, N.J. Used with permission of Paulist Press (www.paulistpress.com).

Saint Anthony of Padua from *St. Anthony and His Times* by Mary Purcell. Garden City, N.Y.: Hanover House, 1960.

Saint Ephrem the Syrian, Hymn XV (4–9, 53) for the Feast of the Epiphany. Translated by The Rev. A. Edward Johnston, B.a.. Found at <www.ccel.org>. Public domain.